my Beastly book of Twisted Tales

Owlkids Books Inc.
10 Lower Spadina Avenue, Suite 400, Toronto, Ontario M5V 2Z2
www.owlkids.com

Published in France under the title *Mon cahier de contes* © 2011, Éditions Milan
300 rue Léon-Joulin, 31101 Toulouse Cedex 9, France
www.editionsmilan.com

Library and Archives Canada Cataloguing in Publication

Delaporte, Bérengère, 1979-
         My beastly book of twisted tales / Bérengère Delaporte.

ISBN 978-1-926973-00-5

         1. Drawing books--Juvenile literature. I. Title.

NC655.D45 2011   j741.2   C2011-900366-X

Library of Congress Control Number: 2010943315

We acknowledge the financial support of the Canada Council for the Arts, the
Ontario Arts Council, the Government of Canada through the Canada Book Fund
(CBF), and the Government of Ontario through the Ontario Media Development
Corporation's Book Initiative for our publishing activities.

Manufactured by C & C Offset Printing Co.
Manufactured in Shenzhen, China in March 2011
Job #2101275R5

A   B   C   D   E   F

Publisher of Chirp, chickaDEE and OWL
www.owlkids.com

Goldilocks and the three bears,
Snow White and the evil queen,
Jack and his beans, the Big Bad Wolf...
tired of the same old fairy tales?

Then grab your glue, markers, pencil crayons, scissors and tape, and get ready to give them a makeover!

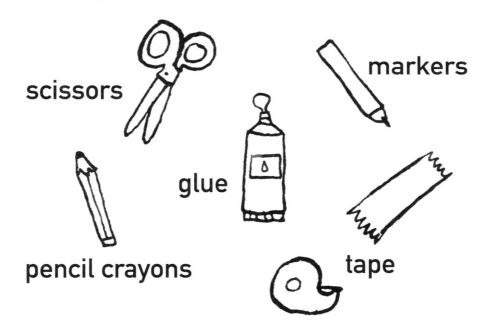

scissors

markers

pencil crayons

glue

tape

So follow each instruction and let your imagination go!

It's time to make up your own fairy tales!

Mess up Cinderella's **ballgown**.

Hansel and Gretel have eaten the witch's gingerbread house.
Draw lots of cavities in their **teeth**.

Snow White has got a bad sunburn. Color her red.

Puss in Boots is on vacation. Draw him some **sandals**.

The Big Bad Wolf has opened a **butcher shop**.

Draw 3 sausages, 3 hams, and 6 pork chops.

Draw an **escalator** to help Jack climb to the top of the beanstalk.

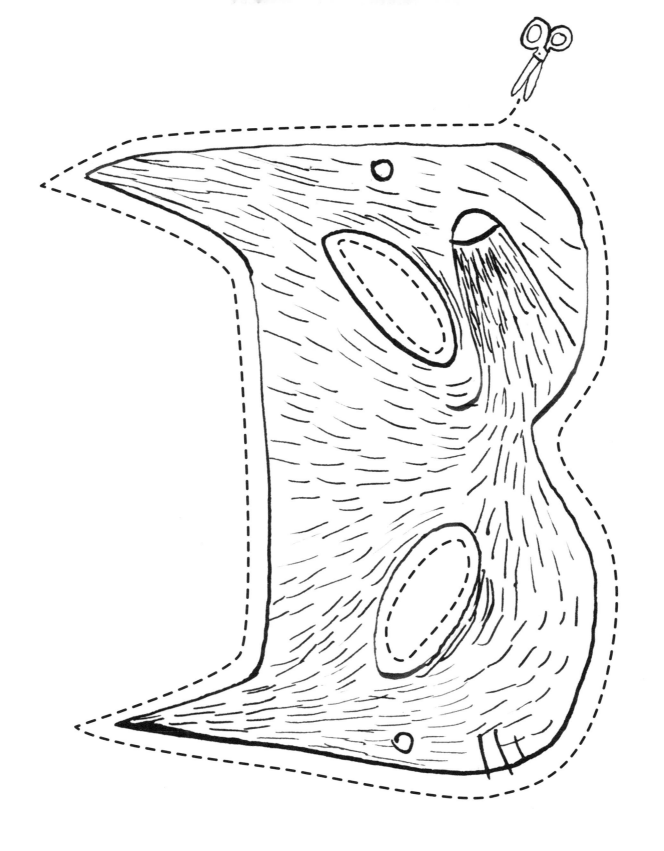

Color in the wolf mask, cut it out along the dotted lines, then go scare your **grandmother**.

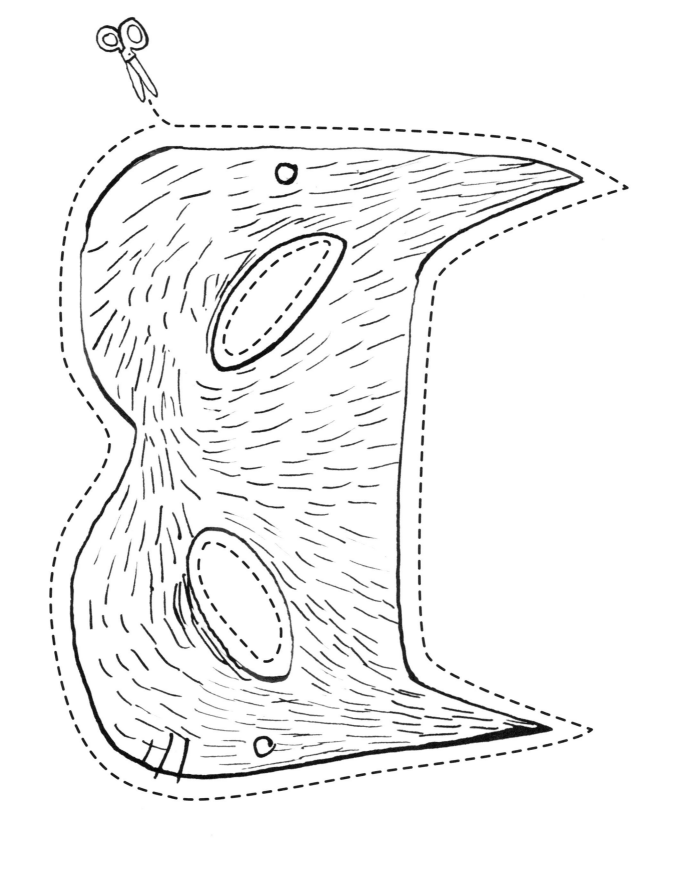

Draw everything you hate to eat in Goldilocks's soup.

Draw the **flies** flying around this ogre's stinky feet.

Draw Chicken Little on the potty.

Sleeping Beauty has been sleeping for a hundred years.

Quick, help her find the **toilet!**

Draw Little **Hairy** Riding Hood.

Cut, rip and crumple the **beautiful dresses**
Cinderella's nasty stepsisters are wearing.

Connect the dots to see who is hiding in the forest.

Oh! What a **handsome** prince!

Now turn him into a **toad!**

Draw the **unicorn's** horn caught in the tree.

The Valiant Little Tailor killed seven flies with one blow!
Cut them out and stick them to his belt.

Give the Little Mermaid an extra-long ponytail.

Circle the ingredients you'd put in a **magic potion**.

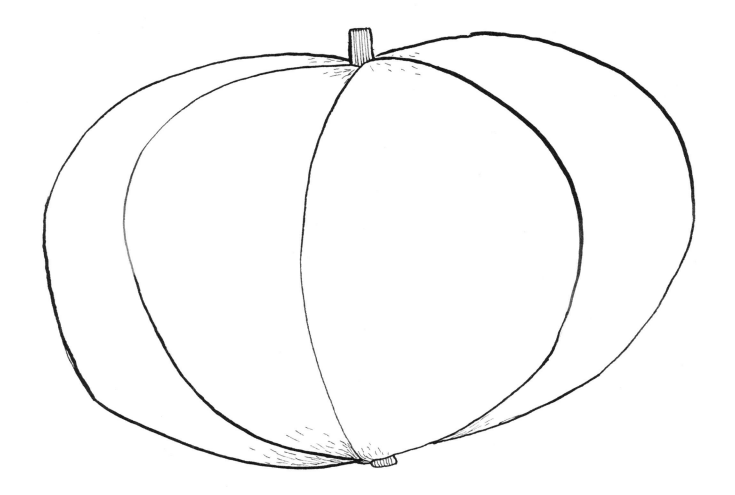

Turn this **pumpkin** into a carriage.

This **peasant girl** is going to the ball.

 Color and cut out a **dress** for her to wear.

The **dragon** has a cold. Draw him sneezing.

Draw Puss in Boots without his **boots** and
Little Red Riding Hood without her **hood**.

Draw a long pink **beard** on Bluebeard.

Draw vines around the **castle** where Sleeping Beauty sleeps.

Cut off the troll's tuft of hair.

Color in the **ogre's** gross TV dinner.

Draw a **brick** fight

between the Big Bad Wolf and the Pig.

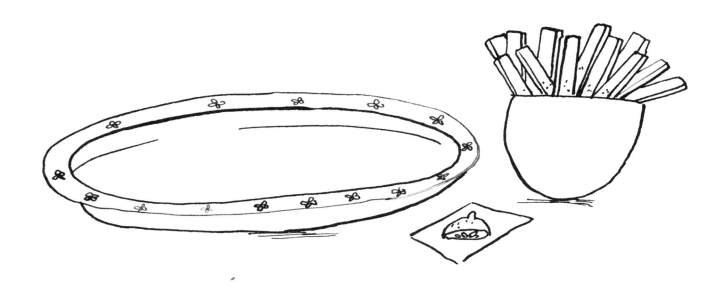

Draw yourself a fairy tale **burger** with as many toppings as you like!

Draw Cinderella's glass **slippers**…filled with worms.

Connect the dots to see what a modern witch flies on.

Now draw **where** she's going.

Help Alice paint the evil queen's **roses** using ugly colors.

The hen has laid some **golden eggs**. Put 3 eggs in **Jack's** basket, 4 eggs in his **mother's** basket, and none in the **giant's** basket.

Hansel bought a GPS.

Help him find his way **home**.

Draw a house of **vegetables** around Hansel and Gretel.

Make **shorts** for the Valiant Little Tailor.

Draw Little Red Riding Hood after the Wolf threw her up.

Put some **lipstick** on the toad's **lips**.

Then turn the page so he can **kiss** the princess.

The toad says, "Thanks!" Draw a bunch of **hearts** above his head.

Rapunzel has been left in the desert by the evil witch.
Color the **helicopter** that's come to save her.

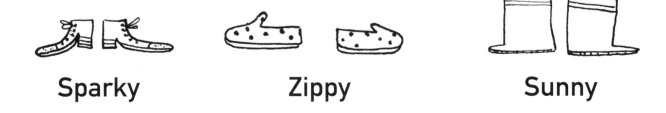

Sparky   **Zippy**   **Sunny**

Draw the shoemaker's elves

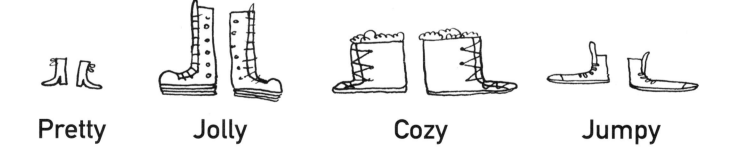

Pretty   Jolly   Cozy   Jumpy

as giants.

Draw this wolf who's making a face like a **pig**.

Color this ogre's **moldy teeth** green.

Finish these

princesses' **hairdos**.

Find the **thief** who stole the key to Ali Baba's cave. Put him in jail.

Snow White has eaten the poisoned apple! Draw an apple **core** in the witch's hand, and Snow White laying on the pile of apples.

Jack is being chased by the Giant.

Help him get home — and grab the sack of **gold** coins, the **harp**, and the **hen** that laid the golden egg along the way!

Color Prince Charming's **scooter** in lots of colors.

Help the three bears get their revenge.
Draw **porridge** all over Goldilocks's head.

Draw more **nails** beneath the wheels of the carriage.

Draw the **birds** that have eaten the breadcrumb trail left by Hansel.

Draw the baby of a magic **cockroach** and a wacky **duck**.

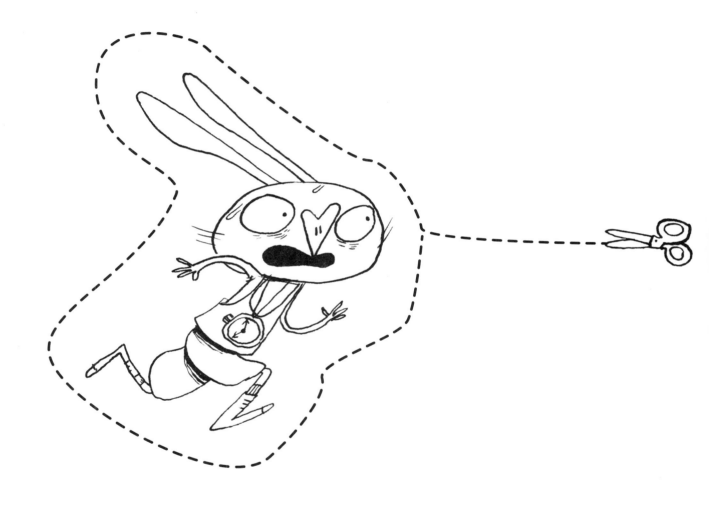

The White Rabbit is always late! **Quick**, cut him out...

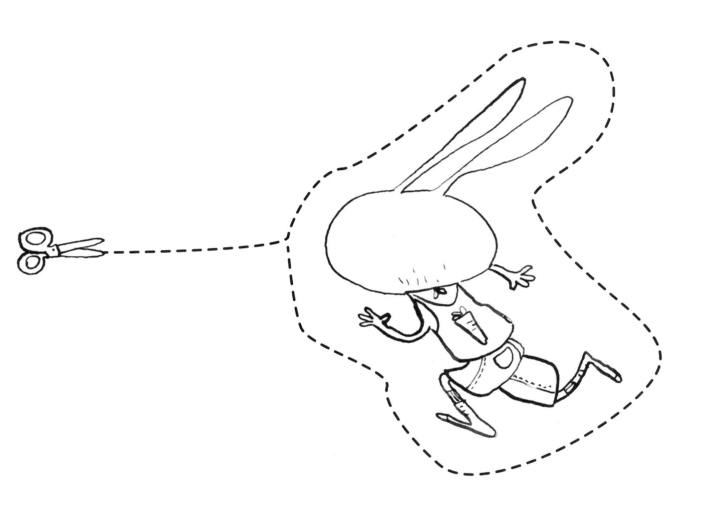

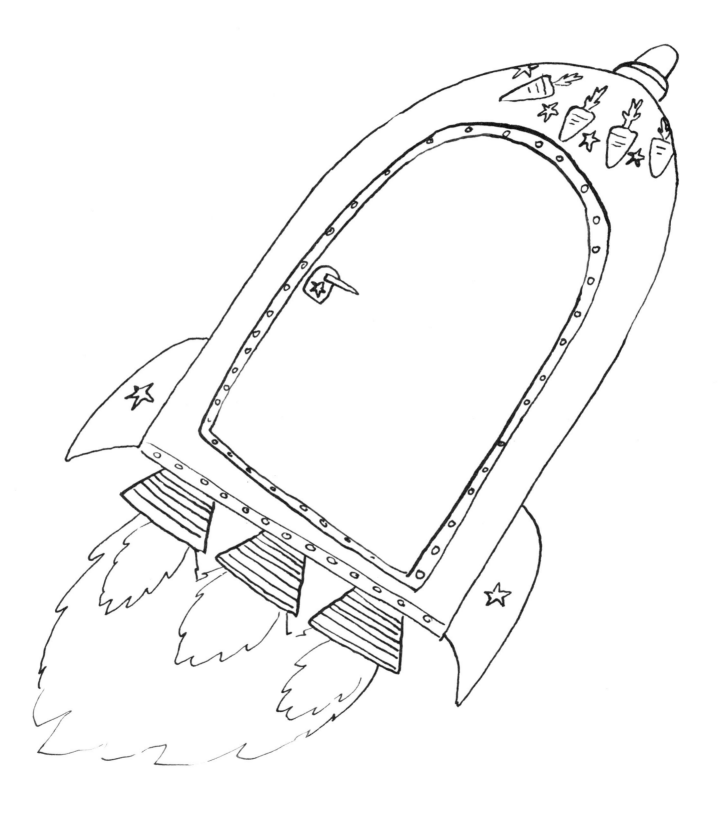

...and glue him in this **rocket ship!**

Draw the bad-sounding **musical notes** coming from the Pied Piper's flute.

Color and cut out this toad mask.
Put it on and give **kisses** to your mother.

Pinocchio's **candle** has burned out. Color everything black.

Using the clues, **circle**

who attacked **Grandma**.

Belle is walking her little beast. Draw it.

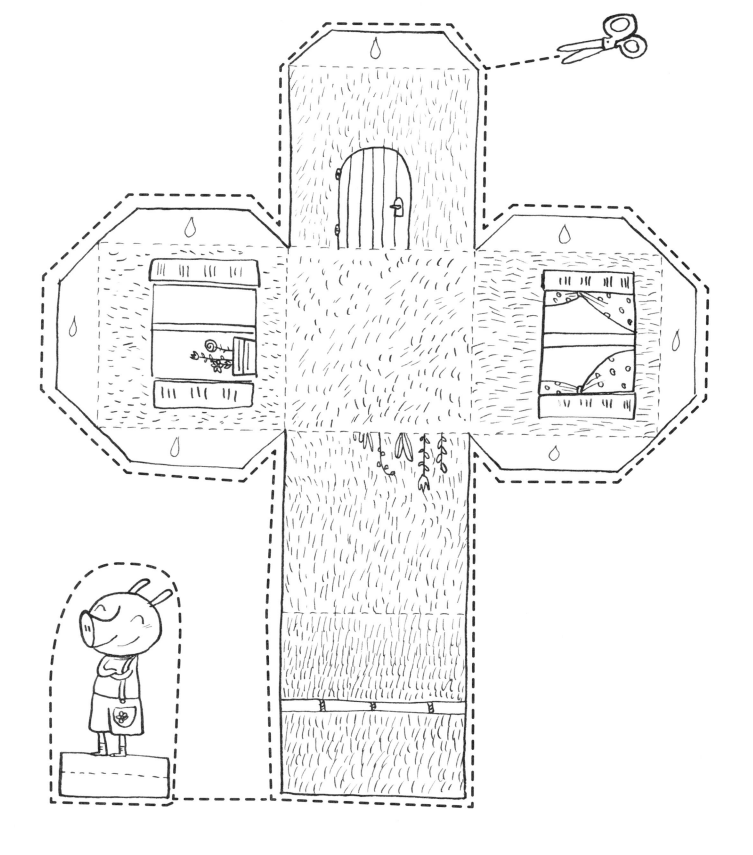

Cut out the **homes** of the three little pigs. Fold them along the dotted lines to build them. Then huff, and puff, and crush them!

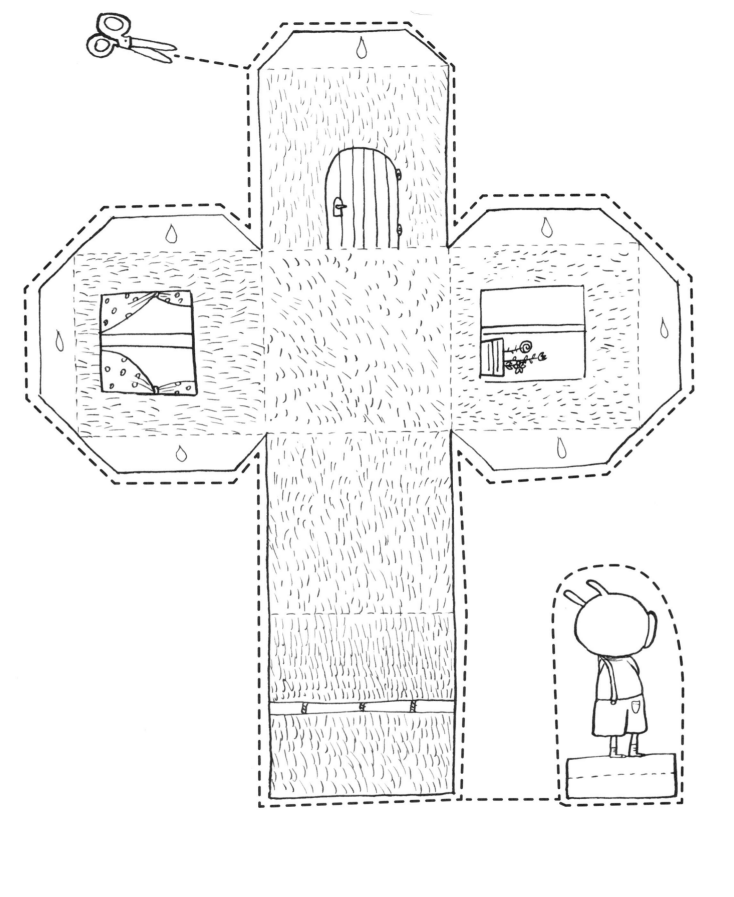

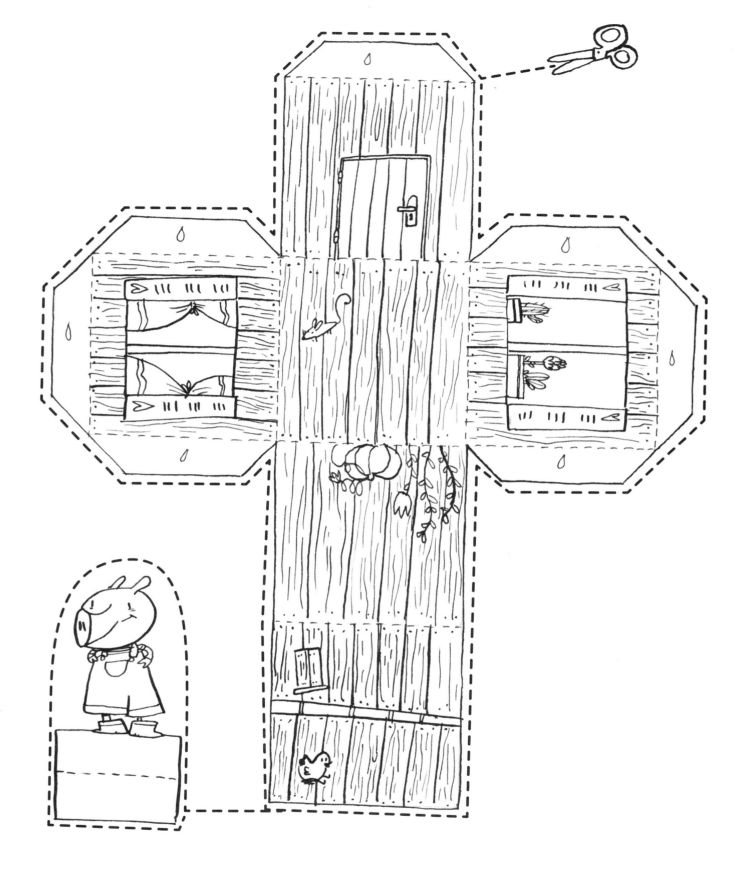

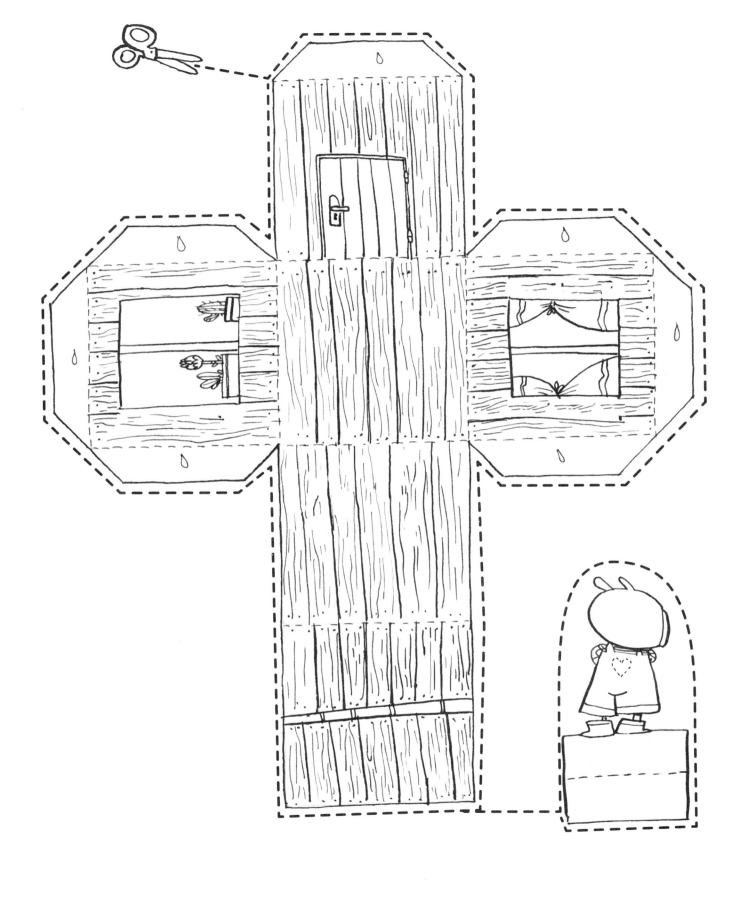

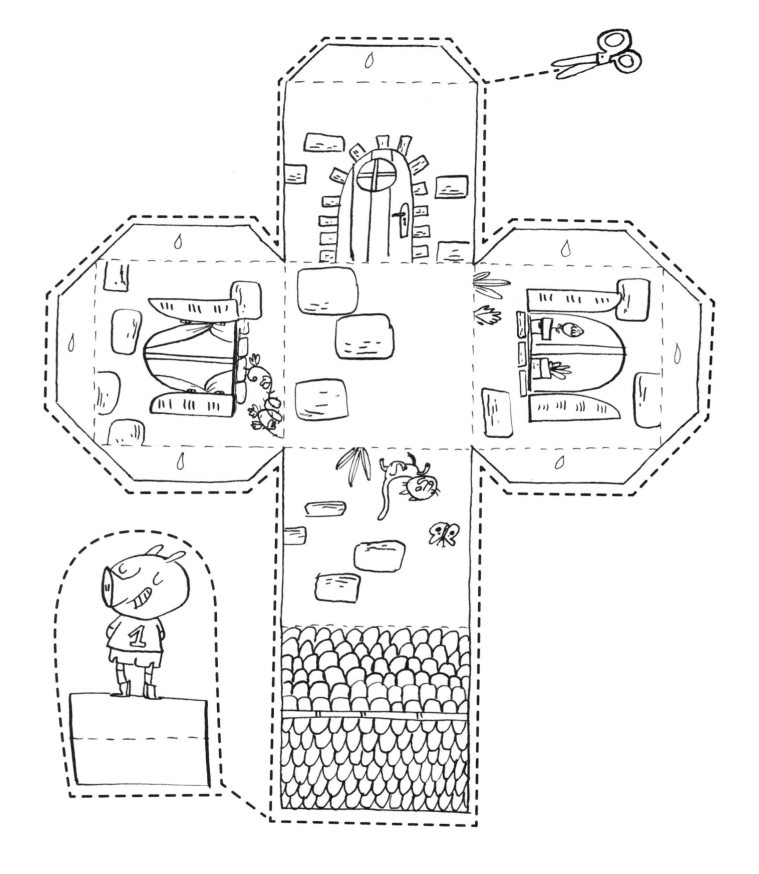

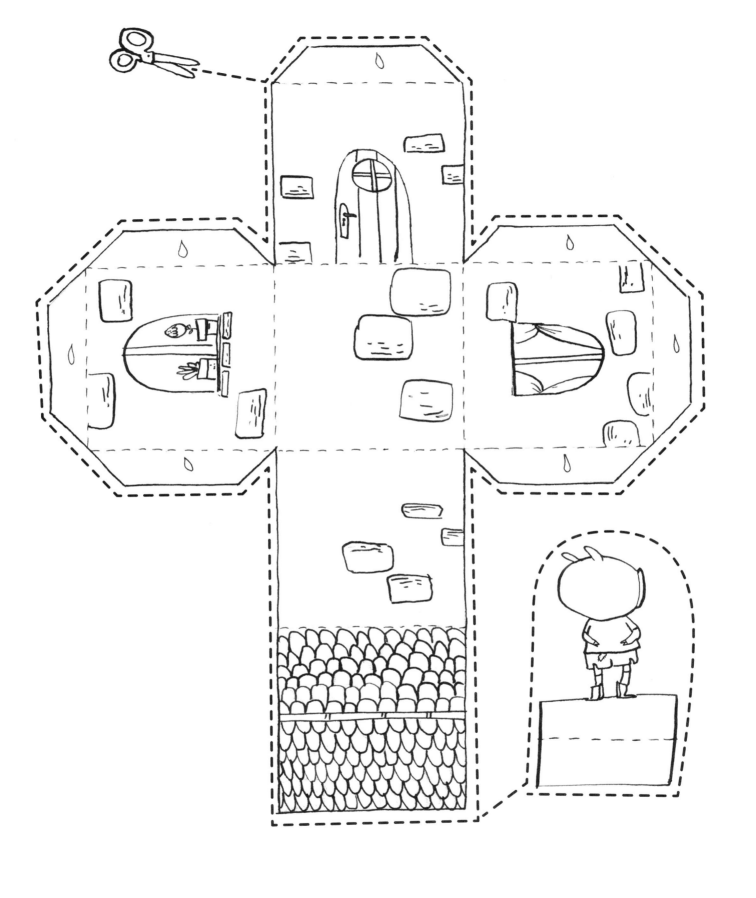

Draw the **baby** of the Little Mermaid and Captain Hook.

Professor

Sickly

Grouchy

Cheerful

Lazy

Silly

Shy

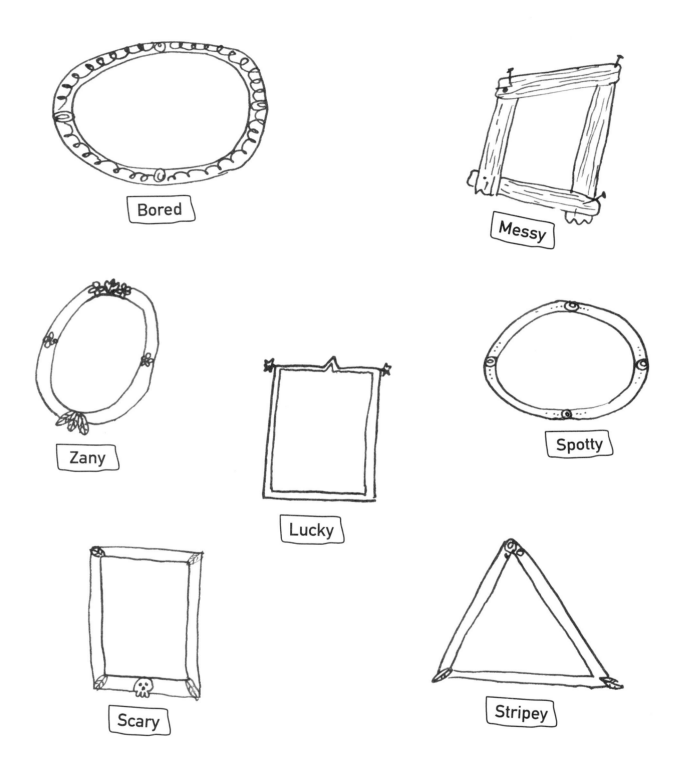

Bored

Messy

Zany

Lucky

Spotty

Scary

Stripey

Finish the **dwarf** family portraits.

The **Big Bad Wolf** doesn't feel well
after eating **Grandma**. Color him green.

Draw an ugly **monster** sleeping on this big bed.

Find the safe way through the desert with Ali Baba's treasure.

Watch out for **thieves!**

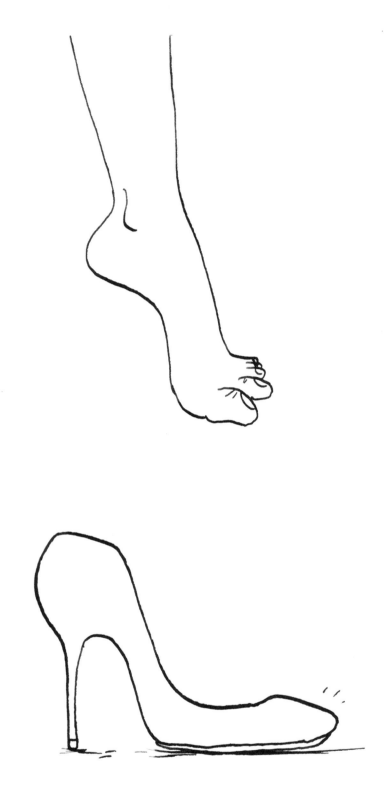

Draw dog poop in Cinderella's **slipper**.

Draw Pinocchio a **nose** like a corkscrew.

Color these pretty **pebbles**.

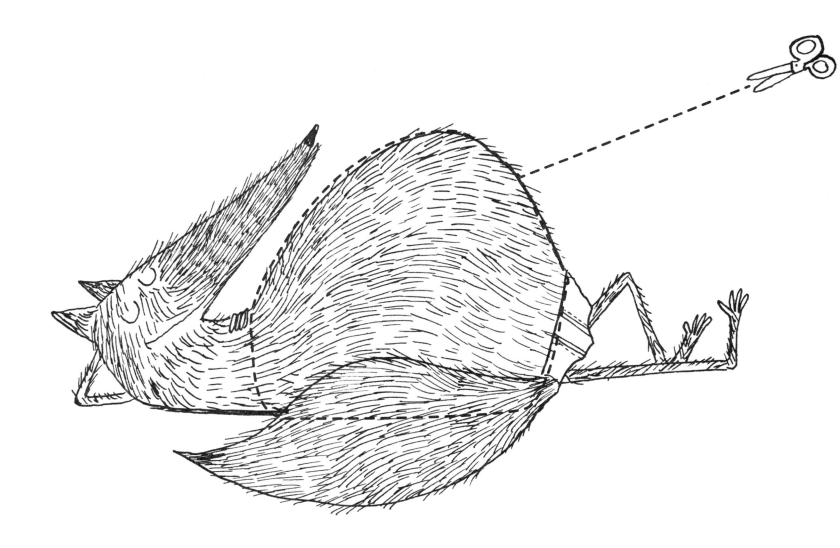

The big bad wolf just had a big dinner. Cut open his **belly** to see what he ate. Now turn the page!

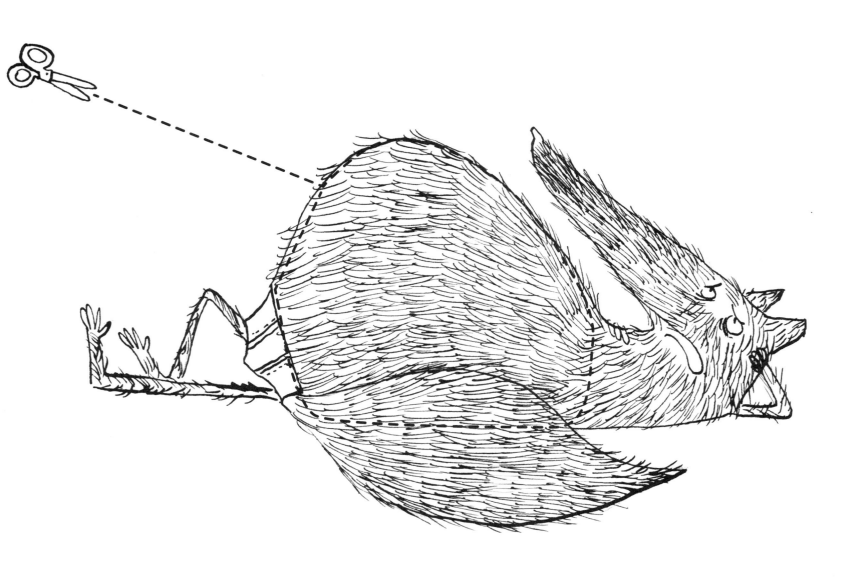

Bravo! You have saved seven sheep. And now, there
are some pretty **pebbles** in the wolf's stomach instead!

Quick! Draw a **house** for the sheep to hide in
so the wolf can't find them!

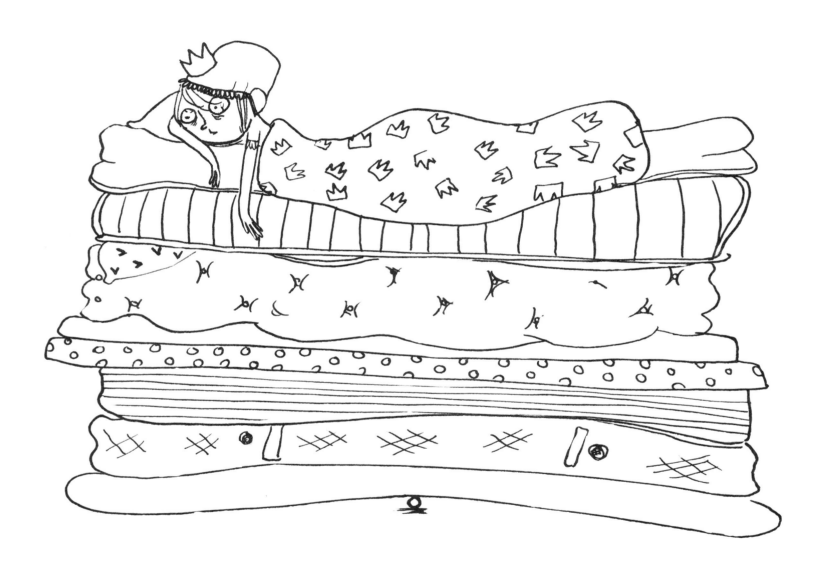

Draw lots of **peas** under the princess's mattress so she can't sleep.

Make Hansel dirty. Make Gretel **dirtier**.

Draw a **genie** coming out of Aladdin's lamp.

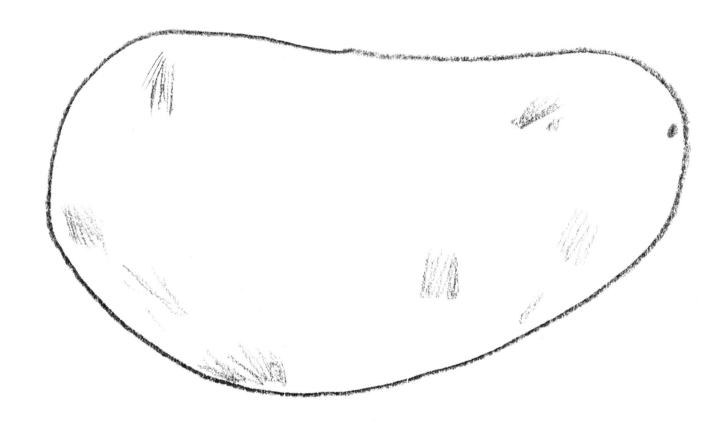

Cinderella's **Fairy** Godmother is out of pumpkins.
Turn this potato into a carriage.

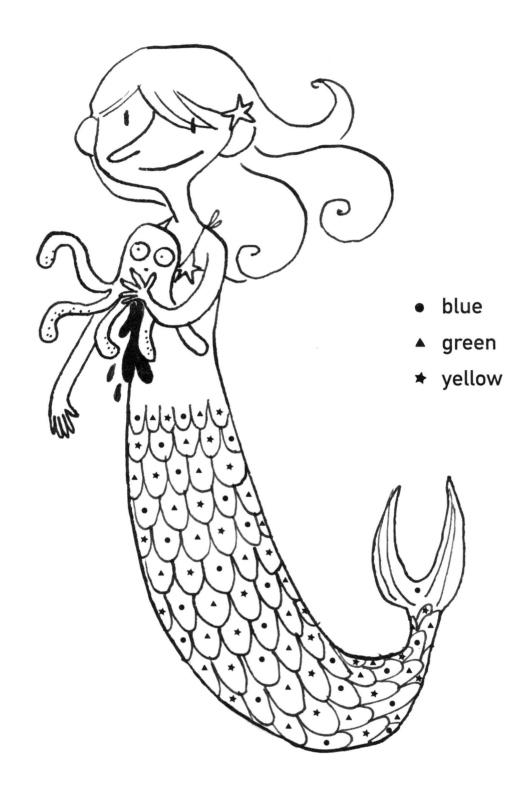

- ● blue
- ▲ green
- ★ yellow

Color the Little Mermaid's **tail** following the color code.

Draw a small **chair** for Baby Bear.

Draw a medium **bowl** for Mama Bear.

Draw a **big bed** for Papa Bear.

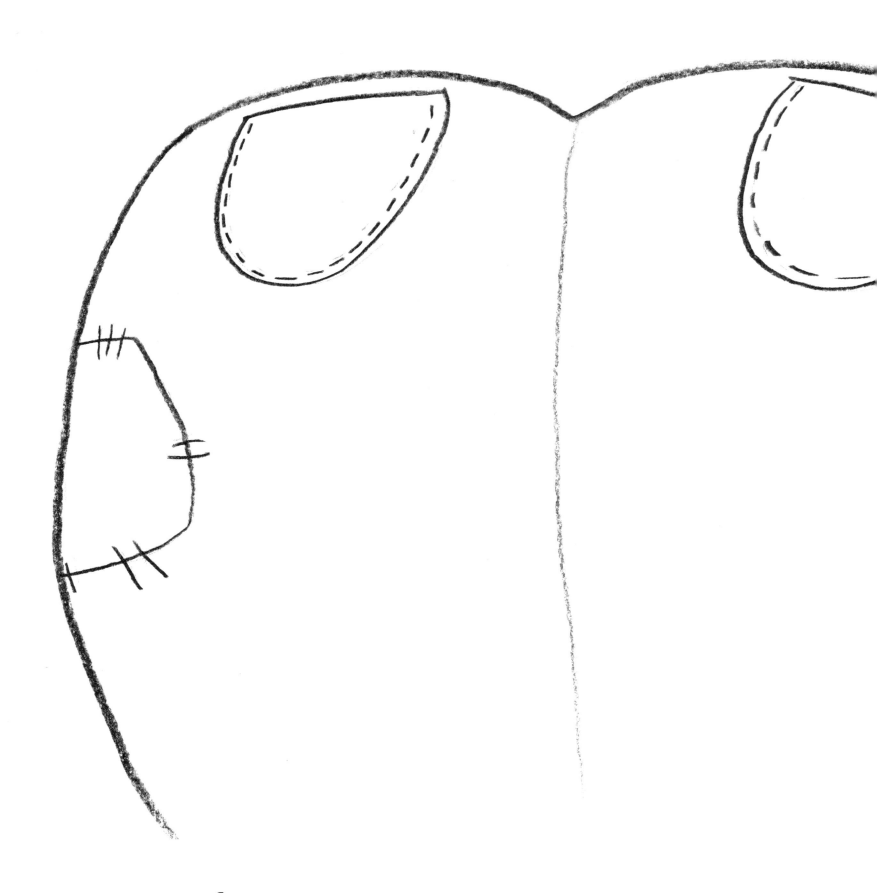

Put your **foot** on the page and trace it over the ogre's bum.

Draw Little **White** Riding Hood lost in the snowstorm.

Draw Little **Black** Riding Hood lost in the **tunnel**.

Draw an evil goblin with **3** feet.

TWICE THE FUN

Cut the Little Mermaid in **half**.

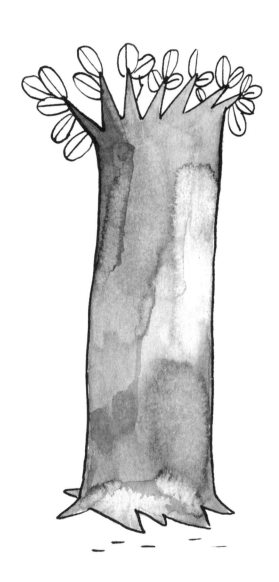

Draw the little red mushroom
Little Red Riding Hood is about to pick.

Draw a **giant** dwarf with a tiny dwarf sitting in his hand.

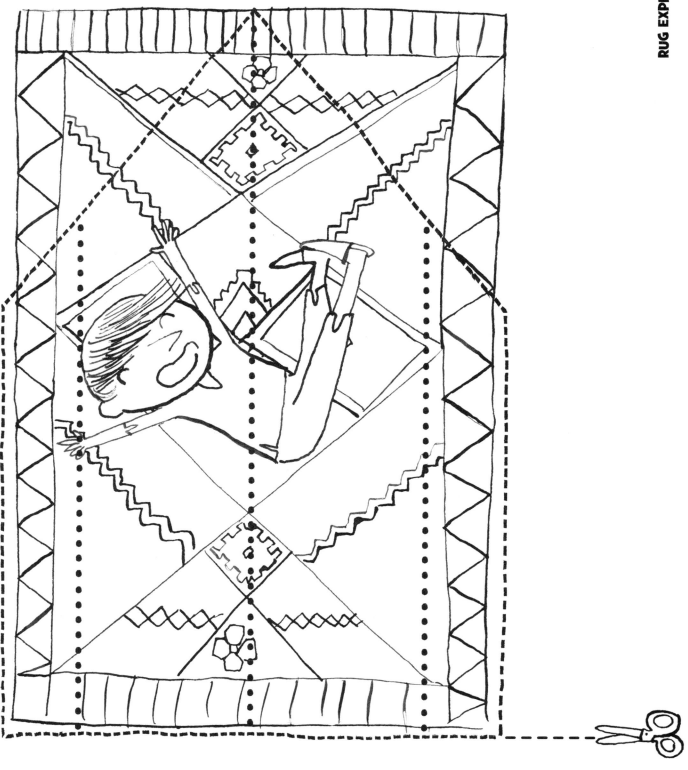

Color, cut out, then fold the page along the dotted lines.
Now make Aladdin's magic **carpet** fly!

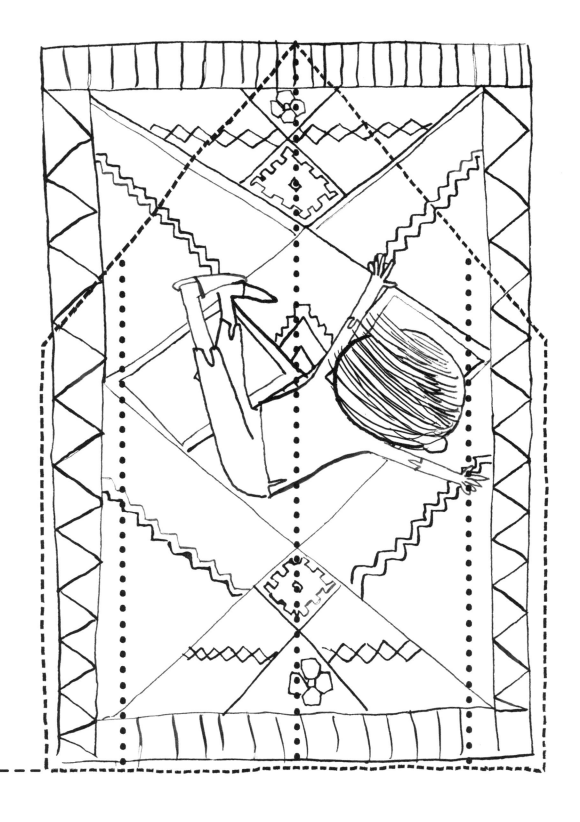

Draw a pretty zucchini in the **mirror's** reflection.

Disguise the wolf like **Grandma**,

and Grandma like a **wolf**.

Help the Big Bad Wolf catch

the **goat**.

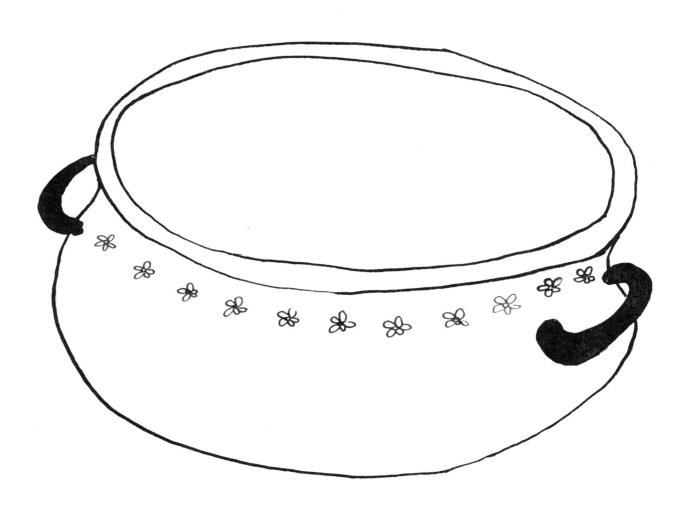

Draw a little red hen in this soup pot.

Alice in Wonderland has eaten the cake that made her grow.
Finish drawing her **arms** and **legs**.

Draw lots of **pimples** on Prince Charming.

Cut Rapunzel's **hair** any way that you like.

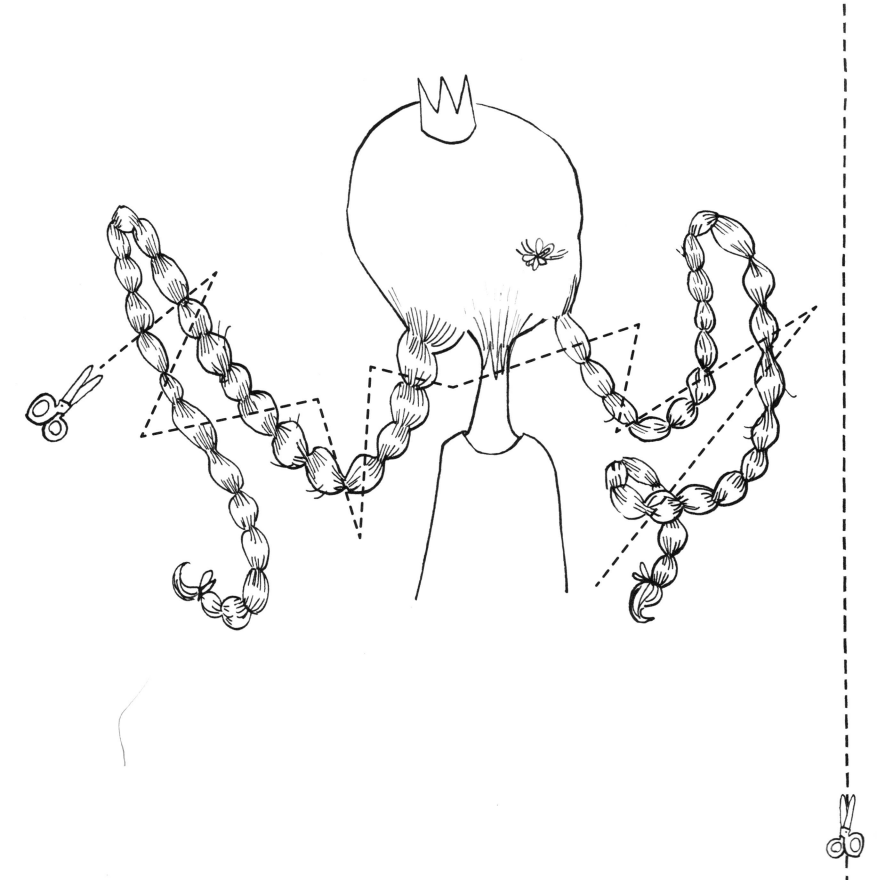

Draw an **ugly** face on Belle, and a **handsome** face on Beast.

Draw an **inner tube** for the Little Mermaid to use.

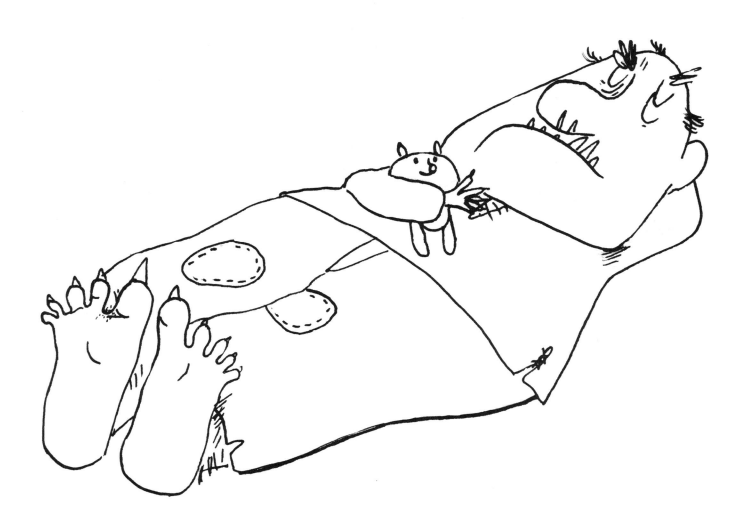

Tickle the ogre's feet with your marker.

Help the Big Bad Wolf attack the brick house. Draw him a **tank!**

Your Fairy Godmother will grant you **one wish**.
Draw what you wish for.

Put your hand on the page and **trace** it with a marker.
Oops! You've squished Tom Thumb.

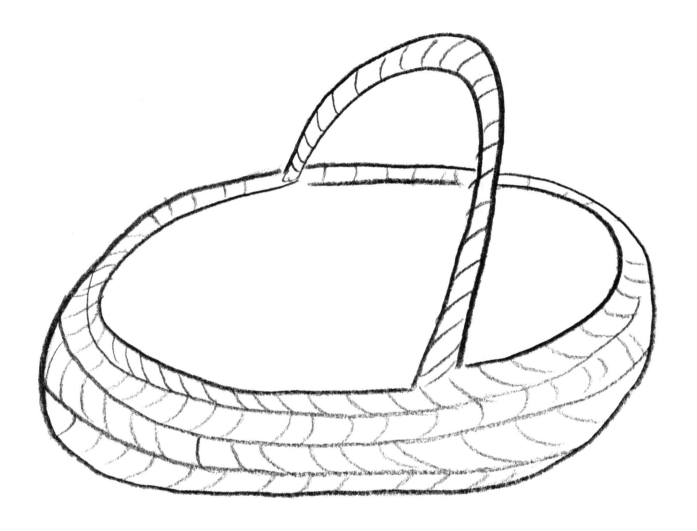

Draw all your favorite foods in Little Red Riding Hood's **basket**.

Trap Tom Thumb in the forest

by coloring in all the pebbles.

Nothing to do. **Cry wolf!**

Decorate **Prince Charming's** car to look very modern.

Circle the one **tin soldier** that was poorly made.

Tom Thumb needs to go to the bathroom in the woods!
Draw a **bush** for him to hide behind.

Draw lots of **dirty bugs** in Bluebeard's beard.

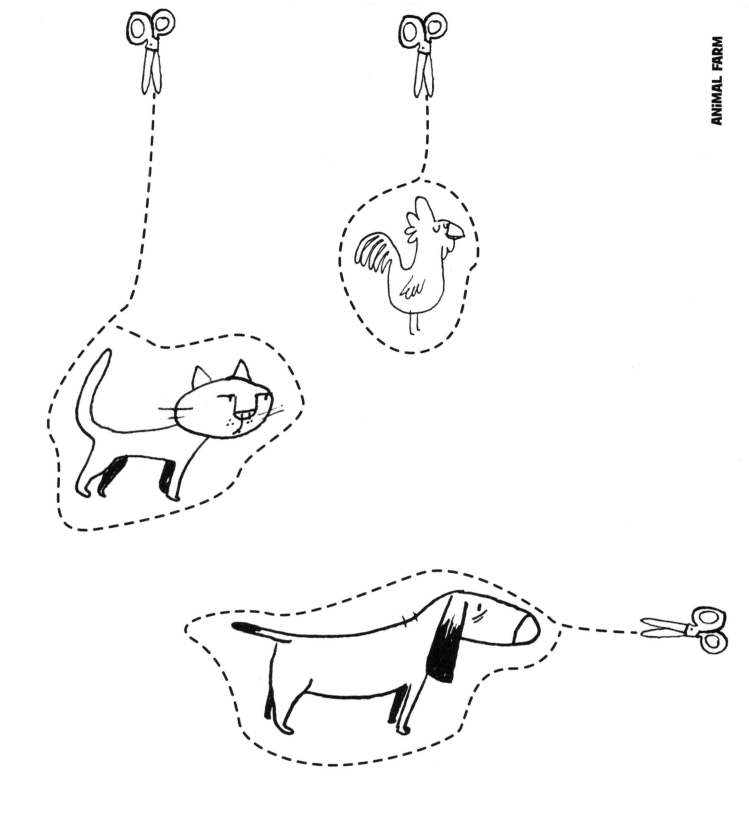

Cut out these **animals**.

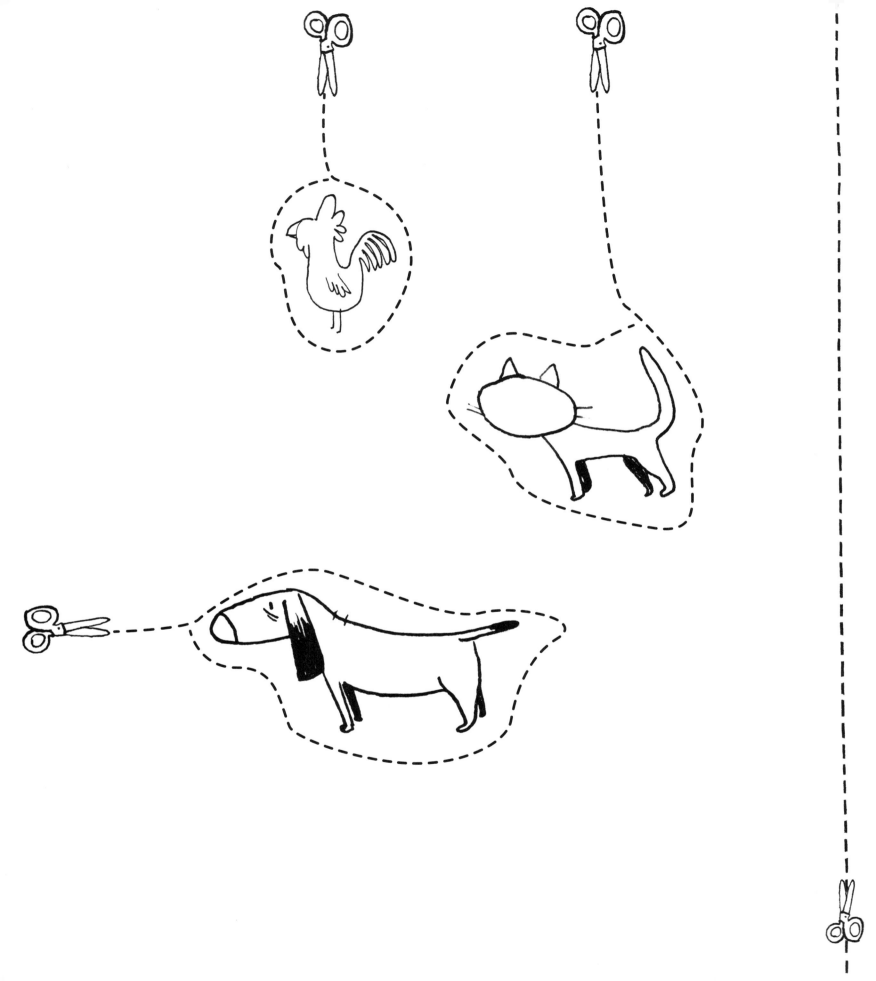

Now pile them up on the **donkey's** back.

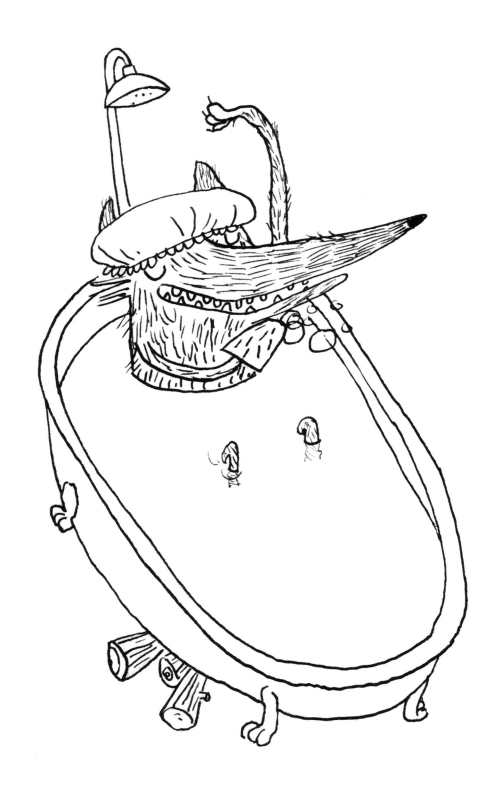

Make wolf soup.
Add some vegetables, and a fire under the **bathtub**.

Draw **rabbit** ears on this peasant girl.

Find and circle **Puss in Boots**.

Now give all of the animals **umbrellas** and make it rain!

Draw the Three Little Pigs as **bacon strips**.

Rules of the Game

The aim of the game is to group together as many families as possible. For two or more players.

1. The Fairy Tale Families are numbered from 1 to 4. Each player is dealt 3 cards. The leftover cards are placed in a pile in the middle, face down.

2. The first player asks another player for a card in one of the families that he or she is trying to group. For example, "In the Snow White family, I need number 2." Players must give up the cards if they have them.

3. If the other player doesn't have the card, he or she says "Ribbit," then the first player gets to choose a card from the center pile. That player's turn continues if he or she picks the card asked for. If not, the next player gets a turn. The person who collects the most families wins.

Color and cut out your very own
Seven Fairy Tale Families game.

1
The Three
Little Pigs

The First Little Pig

2
The Three
Little Pigs

The Second Little Pig

3
The Three
Little Pigs

The Third Little Pig

4
The Three
Little Pigs

The Big Bad Wolf

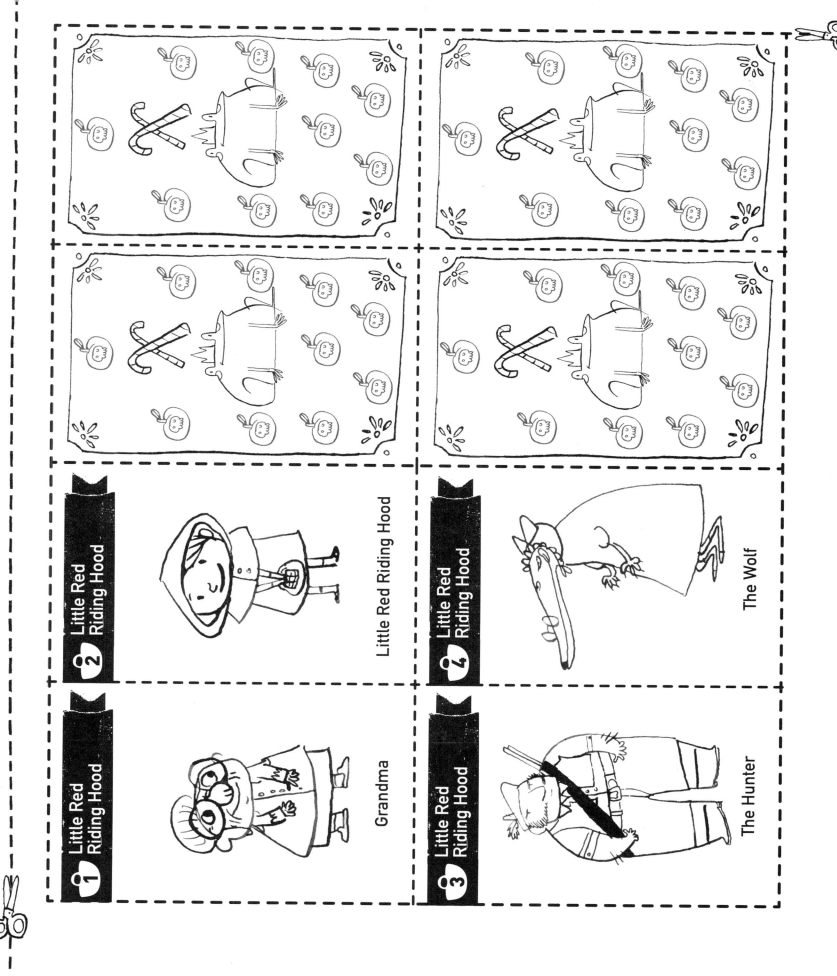

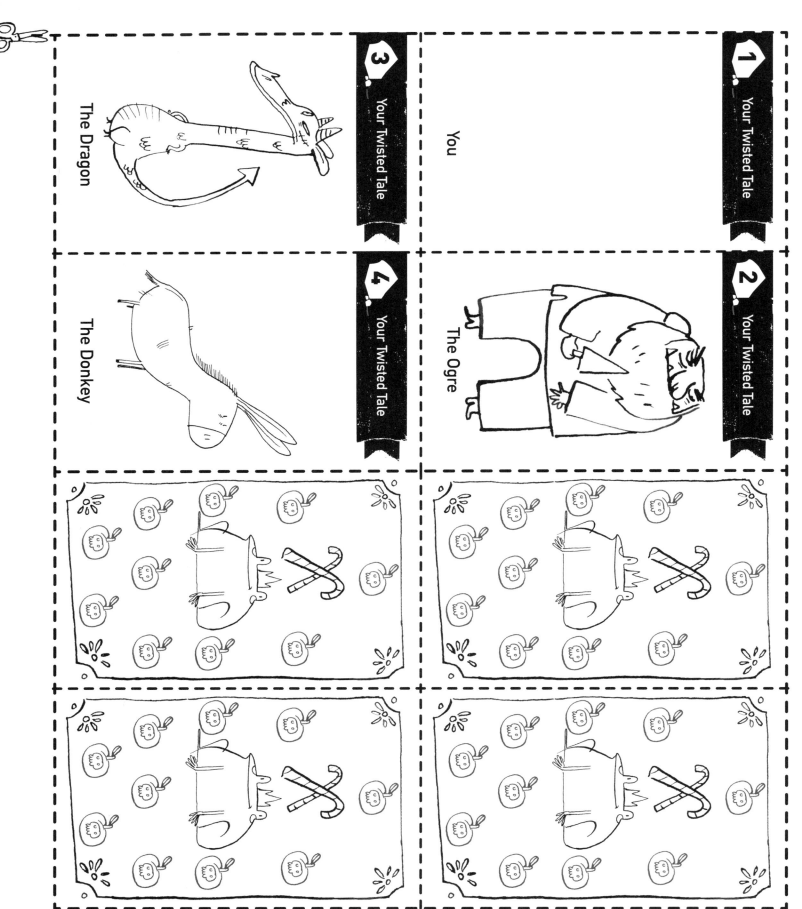

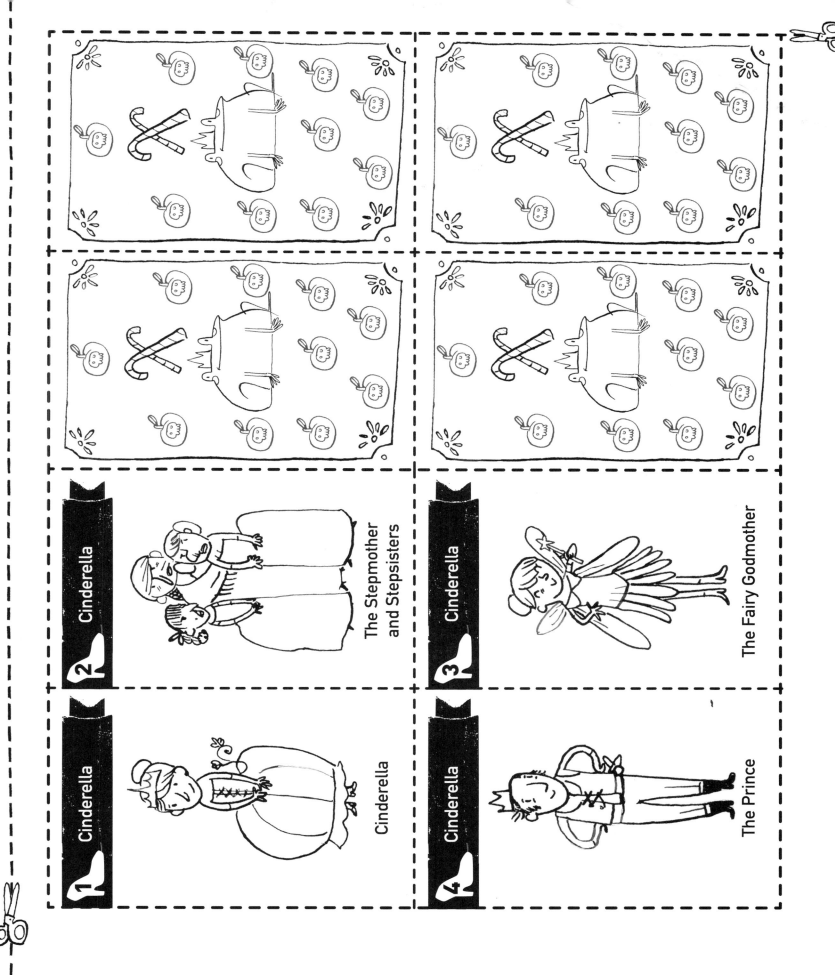

Cinderella

1 Cinderella

2 The Stepmother and Stepsisters

3 The Fairy Godmother

4 The Prince

1 Snow White

Snow White

2 Snow White

The Witch

3 Snow White

The Prince

4 Snow White

The Seven Dwarfs

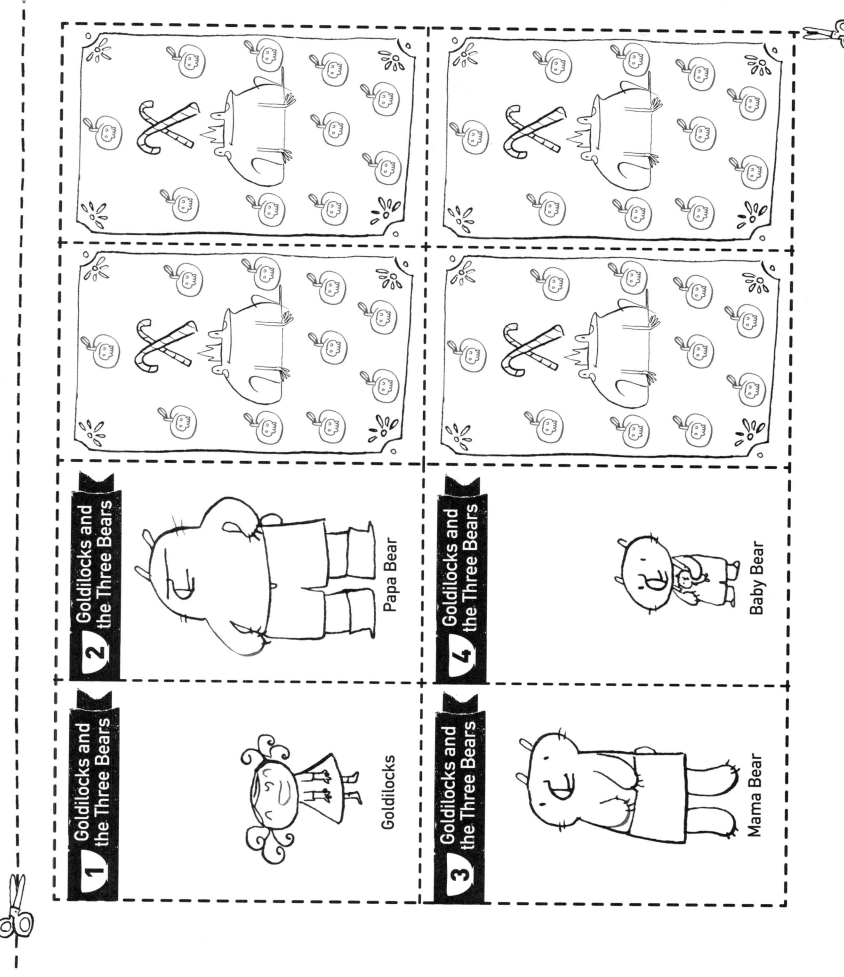

Goldilocks and the Three Bears

1 Goldilocks

2 Papa Bear

3 Mama Bear

4 Baby Bear